Dan,
Congrats on a successful residency year. Thanks for all of your contributions to our PLC - I can't wait to see all the amazing things you will do for your future students!
Rachele

Dan - it's really been a pleasure to coach you this year and support you this spring. You've grown so much and more importantly, I know that trajectory will continue! Thanks for sharing about the "Dan-gent" as well!
Tracy

The Art of Being Human

Learning to live a meaningful, joyful life

By Joanna Hambidge & Carlie Barnhart

WITH ARTWORK FROM THE STANLEY BRITISH PRIMARY SCHOOL

DEDICATED TO

Carolyn Hambidge

TEACHER, MOTHER, FRIEND,
AND FOUNDER OF
THE STANLEY BRITISH PRIMARY SCHOOL
DENVER, COLORADO

*Thank you for all you have taught us
about learning and living.*

About The Art of Being Human

The Art of Being Human, a picture book for people of all ages, highlights in simple words and children's artwork how to find meaning and joy in life. Based on the philosophy and practice of Carolyn Hambidge and the teachers of the Stanley British Primary School in Denver, Colorado, this book offers a life-affirming way for all of us to interact with the world and each other. See, read, and absorb these pages to be reminded of the most essential and positive qualities of being human.

To live a meaningful, joyful life . . .

See everyone as unique and significant

Focus on the positive

"I'm great at jump roping." - Isabel

Believe
in the
potential
of each
person

Take time to get to know one another

Laugh

Play

Listen

"The important thing about me is . . . I love to climb trees.
I like that I was born on a blue moon. But . . . the important thing
about me is that I love to climb trees." – Arlana

Empathize

Know we all feel sad sometimes

Take care of one another

Build a community

Collaborate

Love learning

Explore

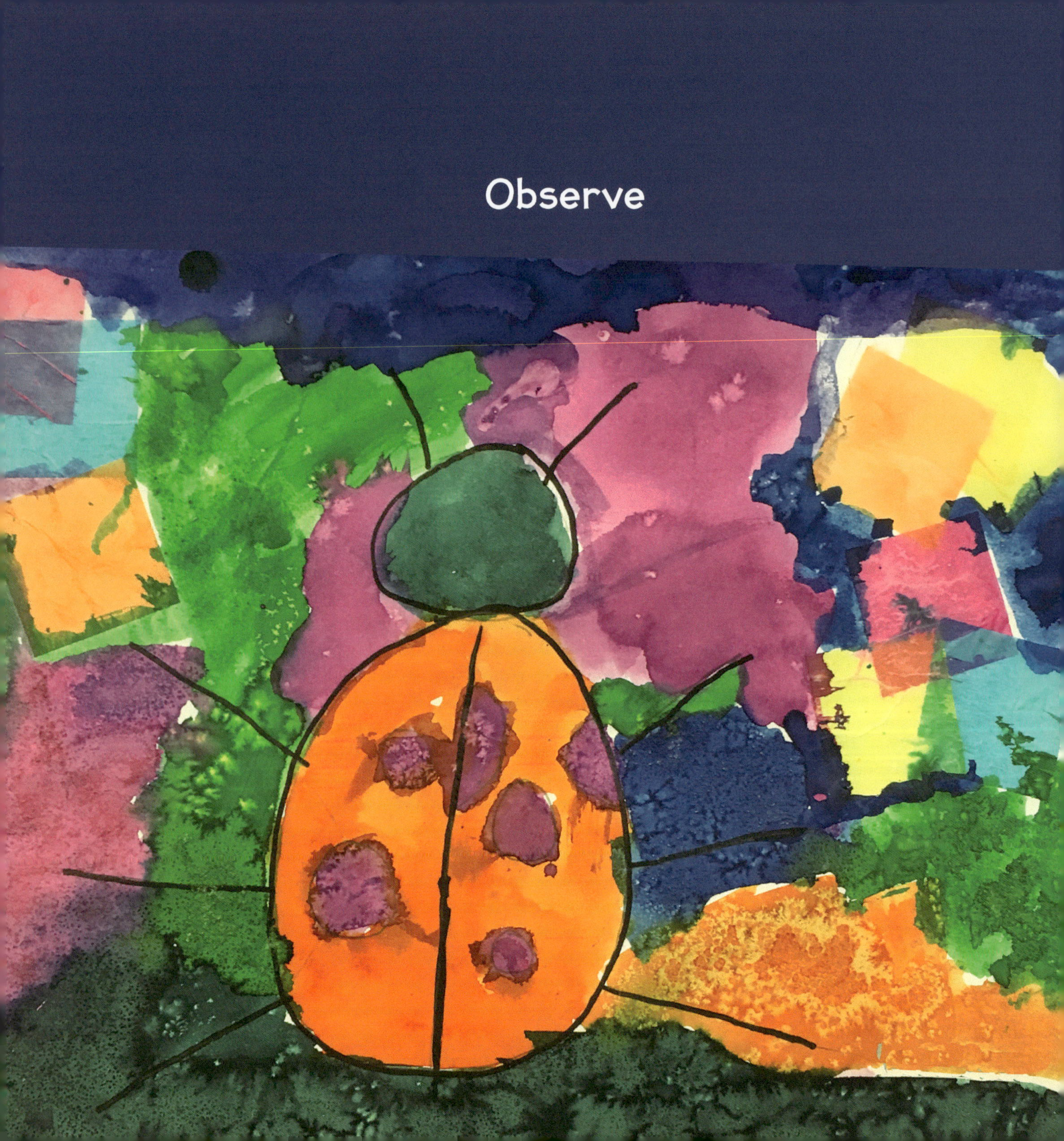

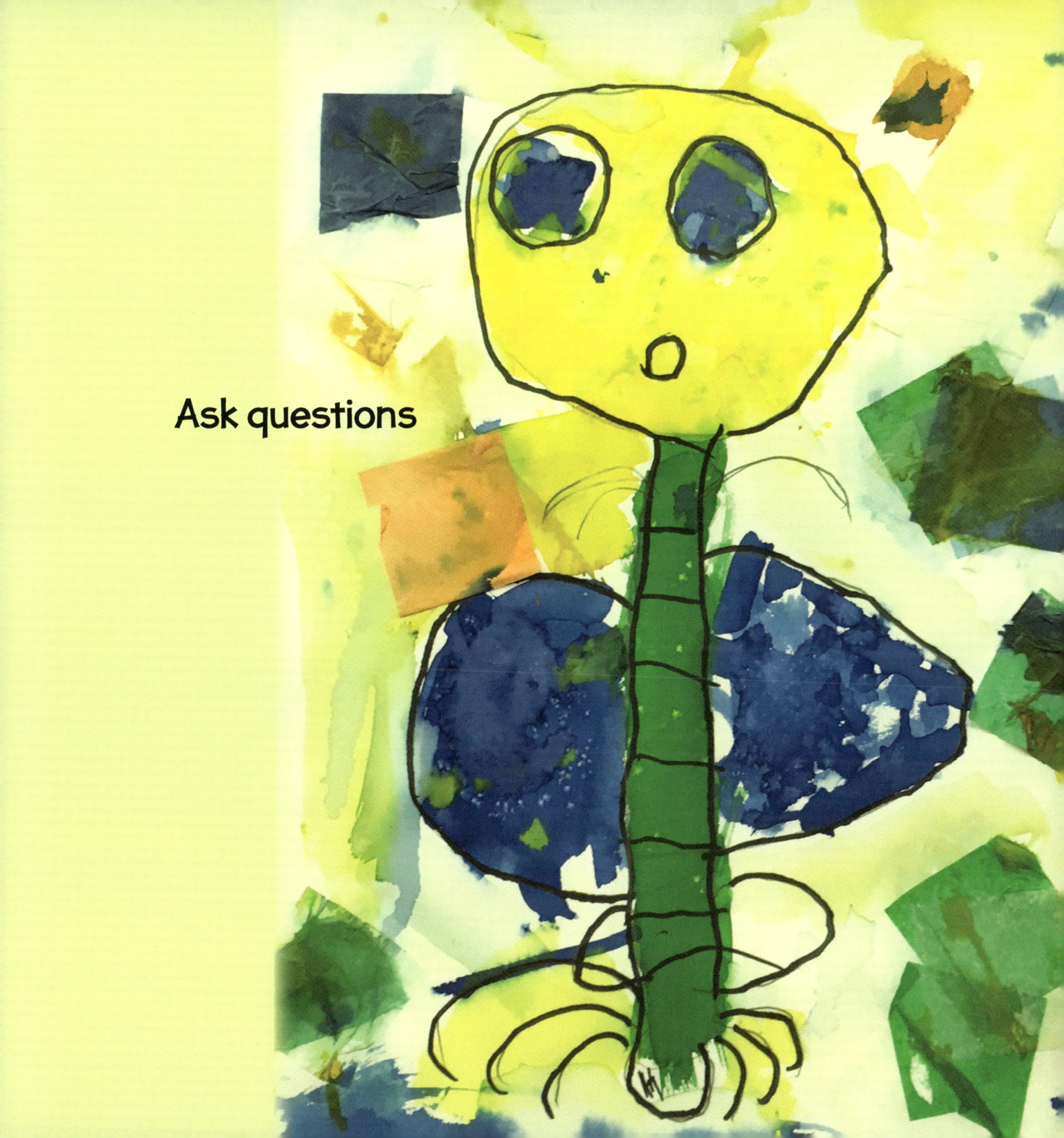

Ask questions

Think

Problem-solve

Be open to possibilities

Create

Sing, dance and paint

Work hard, persevere

Walk, skip and eat healthy
with the occasional square of
dark chocolate

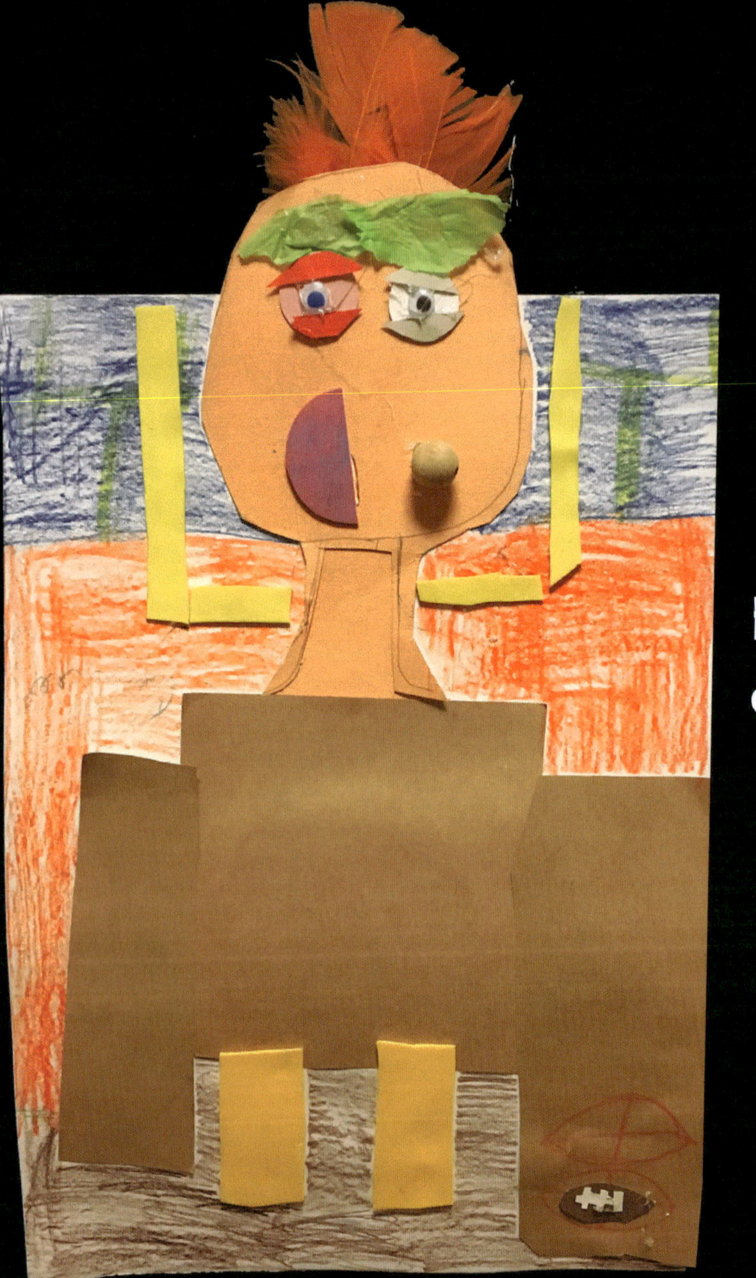

Find your voice and use it

Choose

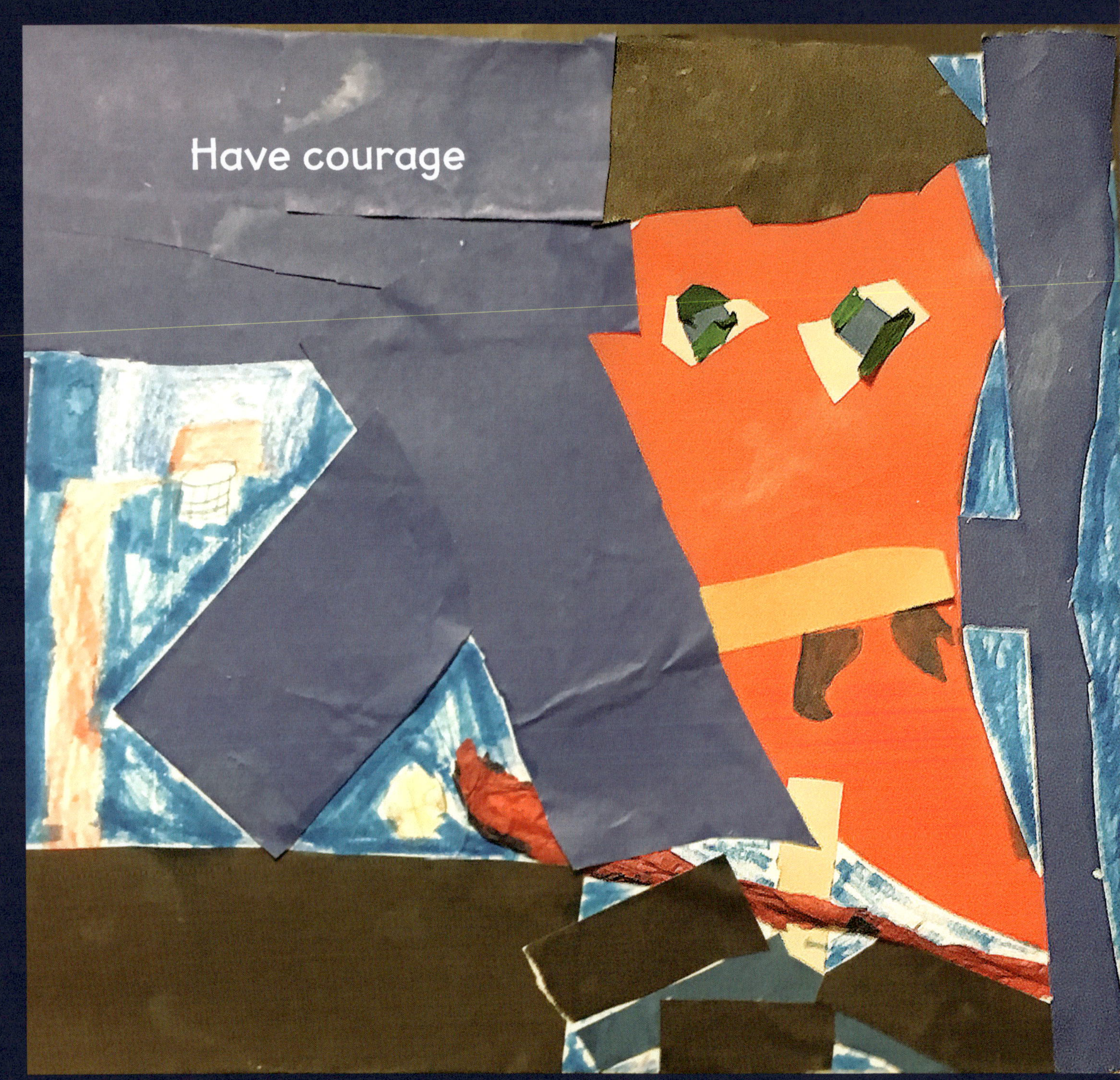

Have courage

Be honest

Find meaning

Be grateful

Breathe deeply

Appreciate each moment

"I'm good at taking care of my two puppies." - Andrew

and ultimately
experience joy

About Carolyn Hambidge

Carolyn grew up in England, where, as a young adult, she studied at the Froebel Institute, and later taught in inner-city London. In 1967, she carried her passion and vision for education across the Atlantic and, with Colorado's first lady, Bea Romer, founded a remarkable educational community in Colorado. She has gracefully educated generations of children and their parents, and mentored hundreds of teachers who themselves have influenced the lives of many more. The impact of Carolyn's life and work is felt throughout Colorado and ripples across the country, making a positive difference in the world.

As a teacher and a principal, Carolyn shepherded the growth and development of the Stanley British Primary School, from a single laboratory classroom to a highly-acclaimed model of K-8 education. She also guided the growth of an exceptional teacher preparation program, involving dedicated partnerships with both public and independent schools.

Carolyn's understanding of the central importance of the classroom teacher made the education of teachers an essential component of the school's mission. Thousands of children benefit as these British Primary teachers engage, challenge and inspire learners to develop their own voices and to reach their full potential.

Carolyn turned eighty on January 20, 2017, and she is still doing what she loves to do: She is teaching!

About the Stanley British Primary School

The artwork and ideas presented in this
book are from the Stanley British Primary
School, a private institution with a public
purpose, focused on growing children
who love to learn and who are prepared
to make a positive difference in the world.
The school's goals for learners are:

- To understand how to learn, and
  ultimately to use higher-order
  thinking skills to synthesize,
  problem-solve, imagine and create;
- To know themselves as people and as learners;
- To develop positive habits of the heart and the mind;
- To value being interdependent members of a community actively
  making a positive difference in the world; and
- To experience joy in learning and in life.

At the Stanley British Primary School, learners are actively engaged in their own
learning and are fully understood for who they are as people and learners and
where they are in their individual learning journeys. More information can be
found at **stanleybps.org.**

About the Authors

Joanna Hambidge has worked side-by-side with her mother, Carolyn, at the Stanley British Primary School for the past three decades. She started as a teacher, then created and ran the school's teacher preparation program, which since its inception in 1991 has educated and licensed over 500 teachers to work in schools nationwide. After running the program for five years, Joanna received a foundation grant to mentor program graduates into the public schools for their first years of teaching. Since her mother's retirement as Head of School in 2007, Joanna has headed the Stanley British Primary School's Lower School and remains a key practitioner and teacher of the Stanley British Primary philosophy.

In her early twenties, Joanna recognized that the way her mother educates children is special, and has been on a journey ever since to articulate and share with others what she has learned. Joanna loves working with teachers to create classrooms and communities that nurture, inspire and educate learners to thrive. She is currently working on an in-depth book sharing insights and stories about what good teachers do. When she is not in classrooms or writing, she loves to sing, walk on beaches and in meadows filled with wildflowers, and spend time with her two sons, Andrew and Jonathan.

Carlie Barnhart is a graphic designer with more than 35 years of experience. She enrolled her daughter, Zoe, at the Stanley British Primary School as a kindergartner in 1986. Thirty-one years later, well past her role as a parent at the school, Carlie continues to provide design work for school communications. This special project was the brainchild of Joanna Hambidge, who invited Carlie to partner with her to help bring it to life.

Throughout her years in the design profession, Carlie has particularly enjoyed working with Stanley student art, as it consistently offers fresh, unfettered and many times surprising new ways of looking at the world. This book brings together two of her favorite things: Carolyn Hambidge's philosophy for living a joyful life, and the lively art created by a small sampling of the hundreds of children Carolyn has inspired. More of Carlie's work can be found at **cwhgraphics.com**.

Special thanks to the Stanley British Primary School
artists whose work appears in this book.

Andre Adams
Foster Allen-Seeley
Princess Ashley
Karson Bachus
Lorel Barringer
Graham Berglind
Bella Beyene
Quinn Burtchaell
Naomi Buckmelter
Adler Campbell
Sophie Cardin
Leo Chandler
Nash Cleveland
Katherine Cloud
Jamiema Ciswaka
Charlie Cost
Samantha Curtis
Annika Damon
Ariana Dani
Micaiah Davison-Tracy
John Degnan
Trystan Deux
Andrew Eisenberg
Yohanna Gideon
Llulario Gonzalez
Vivian Harp
Annika Jaycox
Juliette Jaycox

Stella Kaye
Shayan Kian
Shepard Klamser
Colm Kinney
Parker Kraft
Bart Llewellyn
Harrison Marais
Warner Marais
Isabel Martinez
Inaya Morris-Emery
Liora Nadel
Selah Ocansey
Thomas Prendergast
Elias Rahbany
Sadie Ramsbott
Marin Ray
Benjamin Roberts
Soren Rushton
Ryan Schnur
Noah Stern
Sophie Stern
Jillian Turner
Maddox Thomas
Eliza Thorpe
Jack Vehko
Claire Wolf
Helen Yonas

A portion of the proceeds will go to support the
education of teachers in the British Primary
approach to learning.

© 2017 by Joanna Hambidge & Carlie Barnhart

ISBN: 978-0-9993732-0-0 (Hardbound)
ISBN: 978-0-9993732-1-7 (Paperback)

Edited by Diana Poole, Andrew Myers, Stacey Witt Toevs & Chris Weaver
Cover art by Eliza Thorpe

Visit us at **artofbeinghuman.me**

CPSIA information can be obtained at www.ICGtesting.com
Printed in the USA
LVIW01n1724261117
555861LV00002B/3